A SUBTLE TRANSFORMATION

POETRY
&
STORY

RASMUSSEN

To Christa

&

Family

Printed in the United States of America

First Printing, 2014

ISBN 978-1-312-47037-8

Rasmussen Publishing
North Street
Canaseraga
New York
14822

Pages

POETRY

Metamorphosis

The caterpillar-butterfly.
At what moment
Did it die?
Born of its own
Ash and slime
To fly
So gently.

Gliding transparent
Upon those chalky wings—

Was it ever there?

I saw it over there
I think
Among the lilies
In that field.
It was drinking
Nectar as I froze,
Watching,
Barely blinking.

A memory
I suppose—
So fleeting.

But then
As it passed by
And gave me pause
To wonder *why*.
I stood beneath
This clean blue sky.
I was reading

Ovid's lines
About Syrinx's passing.
And those reeds did root
To make Pan's Flute.

And from silence
Arose
Music within the marsh—
Some ethereal dimension
Whispers truth!

So, the caterpillar-butterfly
At what point did it die?
Was it born, I ask "why".
And watch in peace as
These thoughts float by.

Living Miracle

Living Miracle
I dropped
My lover's white university papers
(absentmindedly)
On a gusting night—
And it was
Beautiful.
Watching as these leaves
Flew away like so many
Birds
Like a hundred white
Flower petals flapping—

Petals sweeping across
Brick walls and sidewalks—
Sucked away as into the endless void—

Somehow
Even though it was bitter cold and squalling,
She told me calmly it was—
(Alright)

Ten weeks later—
I was walking
Cross campus
(absentmindedly)
The papers under my arms fall
And sail like crisp autumn
Through the wind'n air
And into the snow and puddled
Ground—

Ten people instantly
(simultaneously)
Chase each paper now.
Blowing round me
In a paper dirt-devil.

All the proof needed
To know the truth of
Miracle.

What is Space?

Fields of Father Saturn
That eat the space between
Each point of fire.

I ask is space
The space between
Each point of fire?

Or is space
The field behind
That shifts, a shadow boundless
In time?

Hungry are Fathers
To chase their suns
Across these shifting fields.

No orientation or golden sexton
To tell them how they move
If they move at all.

When I search for words
I am the quiet stillness
That brings back
Light upon the world.

Scream out "God"
In the wilderness
And marvel,
Become filled with
The Wonder
At the Silence—

It responds in
EVERYTHING.
But it says nothing.

Let this EMPTINESS
Fill you up.

You don't have to
BELIEVE.
You don't have to
SEE.
Just let it
BE, and

Let this EMPTINESS
Fill you up.

**Thoughts on plants,
And if I should water them.**

The cat's chewing
My plant again.
And this morning
I picked the tinniest
Flower that grew
From a bush
Outside the library.

The Tragedy of a Three-Dimensional Being in the Flat World.

As my body sits in the flat world
It learns to resonate laterally,
It sees infinitely in both directions
And becomes lost and disorientated.

My interaction with space is to give and take,
And the only resistance is the ground.
So I lie down and push on the floor
But startled, I rise up.

There is still a beauty. The sky is close
To the ground, this happens far off
On either side and when I jump, the floor
Like an endless plane is rippling energy.

The Potter

Do you have the
Patience of a Potter?
To watch green things
Grow and to know
How to care for its
Fragile leafs.
To balance each species
But not to suffocate
or squeeze?
Do you know when to
Let go and when to
Fodder?
The perfect balance of
the Potter.

Something grows
So quietly—

What is there to say
That Nature doesn't say?
It would be a sin
Not to feel cold
Not to grow old
Not to watch this flower
In the summer sun.
Are my words non-sense?
Or have you found the key?
Give yourself permission
Be free.
Find wisdom before
The setting sun.
But if you don't—
What doesn't die
To be reborn?
The prettiest flower
Within the thorns.
The never-ending
Paradox,
The duality of form.
How it always was
How it shall ever be.
Yet something grows
So quietly—
Beneath the waves
The deepest caverns
Within the seas
Something Godly grows
So quietly—

The Inner Divine—

Hello, what is this sleeping
Monster that I've stumbled
Upon on my dark stage?
It wears my face and has
My skin and hair. Oh—
Hello, hello little giant.
You are me, aren't you? Or—
Better put, I am part of you
But you are found in me.
Are you waiting to wake
When I die? Birth from
The ashes where I'll lie?
Devour this casing like
An outward egg? When
I fight my ego I feel you—
Begging, Sleeping quietly
Within—

The Flower Man

A component cannot
Stop for flowers.
A poet is not
A component.

There is no race
Without competition,
There is no country.

I've put those shoes
Away in the closet
A long time ago.

But I remember
When it was unethical
To deprive my neighbor
The chance to
Build Country.

Now I give away
Flowers and watch men
Crumble under their weight.

He walks on top of
Flower-tops before the
Rising sun. I shield my
Eyes! Weightless as air.

Still Mysterious

Oh— how some men revel eternally in living
mysteriously,
And how some men lust to defuse mysteries
scientifically.
I don't know which I am. Perhaps like Galileo,
I search for the edge of the world, but still call it God.
Like sailing sincerely toward the setting sun, catching
The soft and fair trade winds. How that round polished
metal plate
Skips orange-yellow light off the blue waters and blinds
Us to what may be on the horizon.

On a clear night sky, I still wonder what the stars are.
I wonder if our structures lead us astray.
And if gods or ancestors stare down upon us
Across the Milky Way.

Materials for Fashion

A fetus can sense
The world around her
But it is synesthesia and
Difficult for her to distinguish.
Even newborns have not developed
A concept of object and view
The world as a blur like
Too much aperture of city lights—
She grows into a woman
And develops a love for red dresses,
Fine jewels and wine;
A penthouse pent-up life
That's good for magazine covers,
Dating doctors and cash.
The materials in her cloths and
The materials in her hair and
The materials in her blood
All help her grace through the years.
In death every *they* she ever
Had placed an orchid on her grave.
But I wrote a poem
And built a pyre for it
In my mind.

Death—

Do not stop but pass me by.
Do no stop to hear my cry.
Do no pause when I ask why.
Move as Death and Death do pass.
Move as Death for Death won't last.
Unlike my heart, Death won't rest.
Death, move as Death and do your best.
For Death is near where Death is nearest.
Death is clear where Death is clearest.
And Death is fear when Death is feared.
Deep beneath the water, children, can you hear?
Echoing, Echoing, Echoing jeered that's
Bubbled up then swallowed fierce.
The flower falls, flutters, a new bud-pierce
Through earth and decay. Such little things
Do find their way upon the world
From which they came is where we go
        When Death has lain.

Birth—

Birth ripping
The seams,
Undoing everything
To Be.
Birth— opening like too many red petals
Enveloping endlessly from
My hands—
Birth— water that doesn't end
Ever flowing, undammed
Relentless—
Birth— multiplying, growing
Becoming mysteriously
Of itself.
Birth— on and on
And on together.
Birth— germinating
From every seed. Sprouting
Forward. Pushing from the
Beneath our feet, the dirt,
Transforming, unfolding forever.
Birth— SCREAMING!
Birth— CRYING!
Birth— Quietly floating
Through the air, pollinating
And impregnating.
Birth— spinning arms outward
In a dance—

Birth— repeating.
Birth— repeating.

LIFE—

A steady star
Overhead completely
Still—
Light that watches
The Witness.
So many eyes!
The creatures of Life
Watching—

ANYMORE

The television broadcaster
Won't let me enjoy
Life. Not anymore—

Fear makes this profitable—
I can't even thank
God for the mornings
Because I can't
Remember- can't—
Not anymore—

An inward smile growing
Like jasmine on a cliff—
I reach up to the sky
And swallow the moon
I burst into stars and
Mother's milk—
Can't—
Can't be touched—
Not anymore—

I Refuse to Walk on Sidewalks—

I refuse to walk on sidewalks.
I want to be the man who becomes
The ten-thousand pound elephant
In a room. Like a little black hole
That sits above your night stand. Slowly,
Sucking everything in—
What do we lose when we
Stop and say, "Wow"?
What do we gain?

A Clean Woman

A clean woman
Can not be defeated.
Like Diana, she
Can not be had justly
By any mortal man.

What lets her be
With the white she radiates?
What lens is clean enough
To view her by?

For millennia she has
Been called virgin,
Mother, sister, goddess:

She is the full moon
That eclipse over the
New phase of Venus,

She is white rabbit,
She is cherry blossom,

She is Woman of the Chalice,

And she is red and white.

Once worshiped till
Immaculate Conception raped
Her common womanhood:

The clean women
To breed genealogical fairness,

The clean swept women
Of the 1950s,

The clean women
In the quiet dorms are
Dressed in manly suits,
Await the moment
Of execution—

The Face of Beauty/ A Memory

The face of beauty has become
Painful to look upon.
Beauty has a face of Stone.
She has eyes like Neptune that are
Bold and blue and out yonder, bestowed, alone.

Once upon I could fall close
Enough for a kiss
Upon her ivory lips—

Her mouth two steady mounds of stony tips
Frozen but warm as the sun, full of bliss.

I cry the way we do when we
Succumb to the smells of our past.

Lavender that reminds me of her feather bed—
A smell that sparks such strong emotions before it fled.
And before we wake, our souls transcend.

I cannot look upon that face more,
But I cannot find better memories to replace
The way I felt to behold Beauty's core

And that once I combed her hair
I felt such soft lace upon her stony face.

Slow Down

Slow down
Slow down
Drop what you carry
Shed your skin—
Renew
Be like a flower,
Open to the sun
Close petals to the shower.
Forget about the hour.
And when it's needed
RUN
Run and hop and skip from danger
Like a rabbit nestled in fur
Like a fox blurred and smudged in shadow
If your shell isn't soft
SOAK IT IN WATER
To sleep in absolute
SPACE
The sleep you don't remember
Because there is no mind
You can't imagine
but you are
THERE EVERY NIGHT

The Fallen Warrior

The spirit is light,
And we all come from
The same candle.
Infinitely bright.

The darkness of life
A battlefield, that we
May carry through halls of
Radiance, orbs of candle
Light to fight the haunting.

A Warrior long since fallen.
Had turned his back
At the moment of transcendence.
Pierced in the heart. Fire
Flew from his chest.
The release of his crimson
Soul upon the world.

He now calls me astray.
A demon forgotten.
But I follow my guides
In the sky. Little balls
Of Light.
I know my way.

The key is a heavy engine
That is hard to start,

Finding the spark that ignites
What turns my ample wheels.

Coming full circle: when the
Wind or stars are the only

Force that can move immovable
Objects into perpetual motion.

Love is infinite.
Love is life that never dies.
Love is the space where we meet,
The body of God, The body of Christ,
Forever *in*, forever in life.

The halo framing the stars
In your hair. The dark emptiness
Around your candle as a soul.

The perfect poem exists before form—
When it was empty and whole
Upon this silent page.

Each word cranes our minds
Puzzling our Resolve for Peace—

Writers must make friends with this meaninglessness,
This emptiness
If they are to find anything genuine/authentic/valid/true.
Otherwise it is better if they stay silent.

One:

Mother
Brother
Sister
Daughter
Father
Son
Neighbor

Through this Dark-black Hole—

The fabric—
Entwined lines woven,
A greater image born.

A being presses into this world
As a crease upon the cloth.
True, empty, space behind the
Interlacing. Pushing out this
Cast.

An outline.
A mask.

Death—
The under image is quickly taught.
And somehow, the outer image plays
Upon our minds, and though
It gently fades, flattens, falls
Straight against space-time,
Its essence is still there.
Silent, still, interconnected as
The entwined cords of fabric
Are.
Something pushes shapes
Upon this cloth like shadow.

Pressing, pressing. Pressing through—

Can you peer through this?
Through this punctured matter,

Through this Dark-black hole
And view The Soul?

As a Result of Pondering
The Incomprehensible

I know my immortality
As my existence.
That empty void that is
Never-the-less full.

My Life.
The Life.

The Sun
Roaring silently,
Infinitely.
Standing sentinel
As an inexhaustible symbol
Of both our being and our creativity.
On the physical plain, our father.
In the spiritual dimension...

God is all—
Within and Without.
How do I compare?

Ultimately, I never stop
Because I never started

But how can I compare?

Externally we are differentiated.
Internally we all feel the same source.

And how can we compare?

The bone marrow cell dies externally.
Its carcass fades and is replaced, renewed.

Its energy was not created nor was it destroyed.
It faded into the void and will rise again
Perhaps at higher complexity.

Internally Immortal.

\ **Before I type,**
I am very silent/very still.

I wait—

Breath—

Listen—

Fall—

I curl up inside myself.
Cozy/ Nesting/ Warm/ Buzzing/ Content in Joy.
I clear my space And
watch and wait
For what will bubble-up.

I'm brewing.
I'm cooking.
I'm soaking dry.

An image of myself surrounded by cotton
And pink light.
All in the cosmos.

First before the coffee

First before the coffee's full
The morning is an empty cup.
The rest of stillness
The morning wakes
And sings of endless possibilities.
Something about the morning sun
The angle of our heaven's light
That calms the soul
While other's sleep
And fills our heart before the leap.

The paper boy
The paper girl
Delivers news before the door
I stare at it, quite content
To leave it where it stands some more.

I exit out the other door
To the garden back behind the house
And listen to the
Morning birds
Waiting for their magic sound.
Ca-ca-chick-a-dee
In this moment
We are free.

Pottery

It's formed by my hands
But not really—
It comes from the earth
Yet not truly—
Like the stone of magma
Summoned from the core.
And I collect this sediment
By my river ways—
Folded, twisted and spun.
The Fire of my Consciousness.
A Metamorphosis.

I've seen it on Murano
Passed down the generations.
Glass forming *lampadario*
Set to light in my
Sala da pranzo.
Perfection by human hands—

I've seen it at a
Tea Ceremony.
Two in ritual silence.

I went to college

I went to college
But wasn't educated
Until I saw my
Presence.

Light handed me
The Key to fit
All locks.

Blake's
Poetic Genius
Decoded—

First men fight

A war.
They argue.
They blame.
They find an enemy.

Then men create
A score.
They write.
They sing
Seeking to BE merrily.

Finally...
They are silent.
In Peace
And Self-actualized.

As Lao Tzu,
There is nothing
To Do.
There is nothing
Undone.

Trust my Heart

I know you are scared.
I am scared too of
What I see in my heart.
My demon, blackness,
A snarling dog.

But what I see now
Is White Light!

Light
As the full moon.
Light that lights
Up the Night.

Trust me,
Though I've been
Unreliable.
Believe me!
Though I've been
Illogical.

We may never know
Where this road wanders

Unless we are willing to

See.

Throughout The Night

He sat

Beneath

The Tree

Throughout

The Night.

Seagulls in the outfield—

Players positons held
Pitchers pitch
And batters swing
And all the while
Seagulls in the outfield.

Is anyone giving attention?
The audience is consumed
By their cellphones
Lit brightly
And all the while
White-grey seagulls
Bobbing about their way
Flocking about in the
          Outfield.

Have you Ever?

Have you ever rejected
Your desire to be
        Entertained?

Just let that part
        Of you refrain

And feel the wonderful
        Part of you
        That remains!

Anyway, thought you might
        Find enjoyment
        That way.

When I write

I become
VERY STILL.
Sitting cross-
legged at
The Door
of my consciousness.

It is solid oak and
Carved with scrolling
DETAILS. The image
Of a flowering TREE
Transcribed upon
Its surface.
There is intense
White light seeping from
Its edges.

I wait.
I wait.
I wait.
Patient...

Sometimes it opens!

Time Ticking

Time, you tick.
But you tick
The same note
And you
Only tick it
NOW.

A STORY

Erand's Way

A boy and a man are sitting at a fire, talking. In the not-so-distant background can be heard talk from the village and the gentle rushing of a waterfall. On one side of the fire is a line of orange glowing canvas from tents in the village. The moon is a sliver in the sky, and it is very dark.

"So Papa, tell me again what the last Age was like,"

"Oh— it was long. Spanning all of the histories. It was everything after the great fires and the great floods. It was cold and then very hot, and people did not like each other very much."

"Why didn't they like each other? I love you."

"I love you too. They did not love each other because they could not see each other like we can. There was a great demon, a great fog that separated everyone. They would not hear the waterfall if they sat with us. They would not understand us. They didn't have an understanding of anything that was important."

"Is it true that they built towers into the sky?"

"Yes."

"And is it true that they angered the Mother and she swallowed them whole and gave birth to us?"

"Yes."

"Was there an Age before that?"

"Yes."

"And an Age before that?"

"Yes."

"Were there always Ages?"

"If you go far enough back, no."

"Well Papa, what was the first Age like?"

"I don't know."

The boy looked puzzled, "Were we there together?"

“Most likely,” the boy’s Papa said, smiling on him.

Then a woman approached. The woman said, “What a lovely image, the two of you, glowing in and out. I just put Aleaxa to live in the dream world.”

“Is she asleep already?” the man asked joyfully.

“Yes,” the woman smiled.

“Mama, Papa’s telling me about the Ages of the Earth.”

“Is he now?”

The man blushed.

“Yeah, we talked about the great towers in the sky and about how people didn’t love each other very much,”

“Well, they loved, sometimes, and sometimes very deeply, they just could not see very well,” the woman said.

“Yeah, Papa said there was a great fog, and a there were great fires, and then a great flood!”

“This is all true.”

“Mama, tell us a story about the Age before the great fires and the great floods.”

“Well, great men and women walked the Earth. There was no time to them—”

“What’s time?”

“—In the Age before, people broke the day up into hours, there were twenty-four different parts in a day, but they didn’t happen at the same time, they happened one after the other, and they were all equal. For example, from when we sit down as a village to eat at the communions, that is about two hours, from start to finish. They also had ways that they organized their days into groups, the smallest a week, and then months and then years. But remember, none of this is real. It was all imagined.”

“This is very confusing,” the boy said. “I’m not sure if I understand.”

“It is not important to understand such things,” she said, “It was very confusing to the people of the last age as well. They tried to create meaning this way, but just lost each other to it more and more. There was a saying from that Age that very few then understood: there is no greater obstacle to God than time."

"That's for certain." His mother and father smiled.

"Would you like to hear the rest of the story?"

"Yes!"

"These people, from the Age before the last, were unimaginably wise. Or, perhaps it is better to say, that long ago, we were unimaginably wise. We still don't know what happened, but the reason is not very important, as all reasons are not very important."

"Will it happen again? Will we lose ourselves to this fog again?" The boy asked, looking up from the fire.

"We may," Papa said.

"But that doesn't matter either," Mama said, "because all things come to pass."

"Just like us."

"Yes, son, just like us".

"But like us," Mama said, "It may come to show its face again. But there is beauty in that as well— so the masters, who were practically everyone, walked the holy Earth. God walked the Earth in every man, animal and plant. We were naked.

The boy laughed.

"The seas were infinitely deep. The stars were bright and sometimes shown throughout the day. Animals walked beside man, sometimes speaking with man. We could reach out our arms and great eagles would land, as if they were tree branches."

"This is wonderful," the boy smiled.

"And imagine for a moment," said Papa looking upward, "It happens at every star."

The boy froze for a moment, and then looked up into the heaven. His jaw opened. The sky was brilliant. The sky was immaculately clear. There was the moon, just barely a sliver of silver, and stars so bright they seemed to be popping in front of the sky, which is a large inverted bowl.

"And there is a legend about trees that walked the Earth. Still now, our trees are silent. They wait in silence, meditating. They have watched mankind destroy the Earth many times and have witnessed Mother destroy them in return. But there may be an Age when we wake to them. There are some that walk amongst us that can visit the plane where the trees dance and there are a few in the village now that can hear them whisper."

"But this legend, this ancient tale," Mama continued, "deals with an old tree lord. Her name was Errandule. She lived in these lands and her children now make up the forest of Uralong, which is only North of our mountains here. One day, Errandule and her people decided to let the women and men who lived in these lands understand some of the wisdom and magic of the tree lords.

She knew that it would help mankind to better understand the strange ways of the trees, and that it may allow people to better understand the harmonies in the universe. So she set to cross the mountains."

Mama pointed across the fire to where the distant mountains lay, "and Errandule knew that there was only one pass, as there is today, and that is why we call it Errand's Way. But the mountains were tall, taller than many of the mountains in this world now. And Errandule knew that she must not travel it alone because even during the warmest seasons the mountain tops are still perilous frozen ice fields with high winds and heavy blizzards. She called upon all of the evergreens in her forest and all other trees brave enough to make the voyage so that they could huddle together and stay warm as they traveled, and so started the great tree march through Errand's way. And that is how Evergreens line the openings on each side of the pass, they were ordered by Errandule to stand as centennials to protect the pass for man so that he could journey safely into the Northern lands, to Uralong Forest."

"Did all of the trees survive the journey?"

"No, many of them died of the cold, ice, and snow. Errandule herself died on the journey back. The ancient people who lived here formed a party to bring her body back to these lands where they built a giant funeral pyre and then build a temple over her ashes. This temple no longer stands, but we believe it was west of Lake Orlandis, below the mountains."

"Isn't that why the elder's pray on the West side of the lake?"

"Yes, son."

"What are the secrets that the trees told us?"

"We know that they taught us how to access some of the natural realms that we were previously blind. But we don't know what they were or if we still know anything about them. If we do, it is intertwined so much that we don't recognize it as the wisdom of the forest."

"Isn't it true that a lot of human wisdom came from the forest?"

"Yes, a certain amount of it did."

"I have heard many of the elders talk about Errand's Way lately."

"Yes, that is because it was prophesized that Errandule might have been reborn again, that is also why I chose to tell you this legend of our people. Soon, three of us will be chosen from the village, three of the wisest, to make the journey through the pass, over the mountains and to the great forest to see if there is any sign of Errandule. If she is there the three will ask her to be appointed as her disciples and if they are able to acquire her great wisdom again, they will separate and journey to the three realms of man, the center, the east and the west. They will share the wisdom as pilgrims, if Errandule permits."

“Mama, that is exciting!”

“Yes, it certainly is joyous news—”

“Mama?”

“Yes?”

“Can we go pray on the west side of Uralong Lake when the sun rises?”

“Oh, I don’t see why not. What do you think Papa?”

“I say, of course. Though, we shouldn’t substitute it for our meditation at day break. Let us go after our meal, we’ll need our energy.”

The boy smiled. The moon is now low in the sky, and a new field of stars has shown their face upon the heavens. The fire is reduced to glowing embers. Now, only a small scattering of lights can be seen from the village, as if the glowing embers had been spread across the darkness. It was very dark. The family walks back to their tent. Inside the tent are different rooms separated by canvas. There was her sister's room, Aleaxis. There was the small boy's room, Juna. And the mother and father shared a room. There was a small round table in an open area in the far corner. It was only a few feet off the ground. This is where the family ate after their morning meditation. Off from this room there was a small room to set a fire and cook. There was a circular hole in the roof to let the smoke out, but to also keep the rain from falling in if the family needed to cook when it rained. There was another separate room in the tent where the family meditated at day break and at day end. The canvas was painted white inside. There was a small altar for burning incense and soft pillows facing the white walls to sit.

Mother checked on Aleaxis, and she was at peace. Father retired. But Juna decided to go to the meditation room, even though it was very late. He walked back out to the burning embers, where he could hear the waterfall and distant silent birdcalls, he lit the end of a stick, and brought it back to the alter, and lit a small bees wax candle. He then sat for a good part of the night, with his legs crossed, his back straight, and his mind blank.

What is this, a mystery uncertain?
That with all this life and all these
Books, is still behind the curtain?

MUCH LOVE

www.ingramcontent.com/pod-product-compliance
Ingram Content Group UK Ltd.
Pitfield, Milton Keynes, MK11 3LW, UK
UKHW041919190726
13854UKWH00003B/1325

9 781312 470378